Advance Praise for *Honey*

"*Honey* is a tour de force. Comprised of 100 electrifying microsonnets, Richard Carr's invention recalls Berryman's *Dreamsongs*, for brilliance and wit, but is more readable. Open to any page: language and image startle and delight, like 'Einstein's blown-fuse hairdo.' The whole sequence creates a narrative that becomes, like the *Hapax Legomenon*, a form that occurs only once in a literature." —Barbara Louise Ungar, author of the award-winning collection *The Origin of the Milky Way* and final judge of the 2007 Gival Press Poetry Award

"This sequence of compact poems is musically subtle, visually surprising, and, at times, deeply moving. More than this, though, *Honey* is an ambitious, intricately unified book, part brilliant lyrical meditation and part surreal Bildungsroman. In it, Richard Carr creates a character whose search for truth and self (accompanied by the Bearded Lady, the Poet, the Boy, and the Hapax) is delightful and ambiguous. *Honey* is a poetry collection unlike any you're likely to encounter. It is a wonderful, breathtaking achievement."—Kevin Prufer, editor of *Pleiades: A Journal of New Writing*

"Honey explodes the mundane and visits the extraordinary in extraordinary ways."—Kathleen Volk Miller, co-editor, *Painted Bride Quarterly*

Other Works by Richard Carrr

Street Portraits

Ace (winner of the Washington Prize)

Mister Martini (winner of the Vassar Miller Prize)

Chapbooks:

Butterfly and Nothingness

Letters from North Prospect (winner of the Frank Cat Press Chapbook Competition)

HONEY

BY RICHARD CARR

Gival Press
Arlington, Virginia

Copyright © 2008 by Richard Carr.

All rights reserved under International and Pan-American Copyright Conventions. Printed in the United States of America.

With the exception of brief quotations in the body of critical articles or reviews, no part of this book may be reproduced or transmitted in any form or by any means, graphic, electronic, or mechanical, including photocopying, recording, taping, or by any information storage or retrieval system, without the permission in writing from the publisher.

Published by Gival Press, an imprint of Gival Press, LLC.

For information please write:

Gival Press, LLC, P. O. Box 3812, Arlington, VA 22203.

Website: www.givalpress.com

Email: givalpress@yahoo.com

First edition ISBN 13: 978-1-928589-45-7

Library of Congress Control Number: 2008934080

Book cover artwork: © Nightangel666 / Dreamstime.com

Format and design by Ken Schellenberg.

Contents

I	The bees working in the lush outfield
II	This page is larger than any I have ever seen.
III	Hand-holding at the long stoplight,
IV	No amount of washing can divert the ashtray
V	Huddled strangers at the bus stop
VI	I am in search of the Hapax Legomenon—
VII	The Mother slept in a hard hotel bed
VIII	My insipid cat can only cry.
IX	Design in the gothic city
X	I visit my wrinkled plants with a cup of water
XI	He took me to the boiler room
XII	In the nameless, lightless twilight of a winter day,
XIII	I look down Seventh Avenue
XIV	Elsewhere, beyond the parking problem,
XV	When the river of summer has channeled
XVI	I used to love a powder blue Mustang,
XVII	The Poet said he would protect me from wolves.
XVIII	I worship an unhappy god.
XIX	My handbag tries to speak,
XX	Fresh breath and white teeth
XXI	Everyone adored the flash and tonnage
XXII	The Hapax discusses mathematics dreamily,
XXIII	Grief on the Poet's forehead is a white desert,
XXIV	Thorns grow from the Bearded Lady's flesh.
XXV	The land is leaking away.
XXVI	The Poet is not real, even to himself,
XXVII	There were ten thousand louts in the rusty city.
XXVIII	The card player is endlessly calm.
XXIX	A little bird with wires for legs,
XXX	In the long hallway of my building
XXXI	All the children at reality school
XXXII	I had claws on my feet
XXXIII	By morning I believe in five gods,
XXXIV	The Hapax is rumored to ride the subway
XXXV	Somewhere a dying child
XXXVI	My beach towel a chaotic rectangle of loose strings,
XXXVII	The memoirist is a false witness
XXXVIII	Saturday nights the cars hurl dirt across the track

XXXIX	Through a wrinkled pane of glass
XL	The Boy went out in a butane shirt
XLI	Like schoolchildren with a project due tomorrow,
XLII	I loved only springtime,
XLIII	Lunch with the Poet is all about the hustle of conversation,
XLIV	The Hapax sails continents
XLV	The Bearded Lady says a thousand prayers
XLVI	I erect bronze statues of my enemies,
XLVII	The chandelier is the root of a magical tree. Upstairs,
XLVIII	The magnitude of a corpse
XLIX	The Bearded Lady is a relentless, intricate friend.
L	To whom does a god pray
LI	I idolize the Hapax.
LII	Children on the stoop nourish rudimentary secrets
LIII	The Bearded Lady displays herself on a sofa
LIV	The Poet wears a suit made of teacups
LV	The Boy's deformities require contradiction.
LVI	The ghost of girlhood is awake—
LVII	My words are big shoes
LVIII	We are strange to the bees,
LIX	Certainty comes naturally,
LX	Time, that vandal, broke into our rented bungalow
LXI	We invented shames
LXII	I met the Boy on a hot tar roofscape
LXIII	The Poet stands in a hard, cold rain
LXIV	The Bearded Lady looks into the imposter's mirror
LXV	The Poet leaves not a corpse
LXVI	The artist had time to paint the thief
LXVII	The Hapax drives a glossy automobile
LXVIII	Among cheap, wind-shaken housing blocks
LXIX	I find the Hapax in the bathroom
LXX	Arriving on the scene in chrome stockings
LXXI	The intruder
LXXII	In the mirror of the Bearded Lady, I have golden lips.
LXXIII	I am not ruled
LXXIV	A fly buzzes righteously in a web of enshrined habit.
LXXV	An idea rattles in a jammed turnstile.
LXXVI	Black vinyl legs
LXXVII	Beyond the etched lenses of his eyes
LXXVIII	Sleep, time's lazy accomplice,
LXXIX	Drawn to my room

LXXX	I indulge the Bearded Lady—
LXXXI	The Boy's frontal lobe
LXXXII	The Hapax is at once the hooded bride
LXXXIII	I gather to my cheekbones
LXXXIV	Outside the baseball park, the city is a biohazard
LXXXV	The Bearded Lady is a pony fattening in a gravel yard,
LXXXVI	The Bearded Lady dwells at the beach
LXXXVII	The Hapax is the last dot in a line of dots
LXXXVIII	I want to be like the Poet,
LXXXIX	The Bearded Lady preens her blisters inconsolably.
XC	The Boy arrived in a purring suburban bus
XCI	Every time the Poet walks into a bar, someone
XCII	Under the sun's placid scorching,
XCIII	I distrust sleep,
XCIV	His brilliant flashbacks shrunken to the size of a dusty white pill,
XCV	The gluttonous queen
XCVI	My turquoise-encrusted hand
XCVII	The runaway looks like a depleted supermodel
XCVIII	Maybe after all there exists some barn-vast paradise
XCIX	I share a ritual bath with the cat.
C	In one version

The bees working in the lush outfield
are fat and wooly, more robust
than those found dead
on my windowsill

as though baseball gave bees strength
and the sounds of my sleeping,
kicking sheets, murmuring,
were murderous.

II

This page is larger than any I have ever seen.
At the lightning flash of it
all the birds flew out of my head.
Flocks of pigeons

work diligently their whole lives preparing
their delicate skeletons
for the indelible smudge of the street.
The sky is large,

but it's not their heaven.

III

Hand-holding at the long stoplight,
earrings, chocolate—these
are easy to find.
The haphazard bee finds the scented flower easily.

I want to find someone impossible—the fabled One
with cool, fire-white eyes.
I want a jet climbing through storm,
grinding upward on strong, flexing, silver wings—

I want lift, thrust of the One
into white light.

IV

No amount of washing can divert the ashtray
from its purpose.
The Bearded Lady, clean-shaven in the off season,
offers me a cigarette,

and we share a thin, gravelly smoke.
I want to be like her.
She is a mirror. When she stirs her coffee,
the whole restaurant stirs.

V

Huddled strangers at the bus stop
sniffle at me.
They think I might be a little crazy.
My shopping bags are used, edge-worn,

out of season with each other.
I turn on a vivid light in my eye,
scattering
their skulky looks like dirty squirrels.

Now they are sure of me.

VI

I am in search of the Hapax Legomenon—
the single utterance.
I thought my friend the Bearded Lady
was the solitary instance of her kind,

a shooting star written in the sky only once,
never elsewhere or again,
but she cried and said she was not alone.
I was cruel to forget—

some days she looks like an ordinary woman.

VII

The Mother slept in a hard hotel bed
with someone—not hers.
The light of the mind scatters.
Model sailboats bob on the green lagoon.

The Mother in the park calls her child.
Digging in her big bag for anything handy
she snaps out a tiny dirty T-shirt
and wipes the child's face.

The Mother is a picnic of fleas.
And *oh Honey* she pleads.

VIII

My insipid cat can only cry.
She goes out in the rain,
walks with her head hung
in front of loud nightclubs.

In her day-sleep, she vocalizes,
kicking her feet in the air.
I turn my ear to her
and lay my hand on her belly.

IX

Design in the gothic city
a matter of assemblage,
I wear a massive clothing of stone monuments
and scaffolding.

The street a chaotic plaid of asphalt repairs,
I dent the pavement
where the work is still fresh,
hot.

The soles of my feet blacken my apartment—
walls, ceiling, all of it.

X

I visit my wrinkled plants with a cup of water
which they must all share.
The goldfish, thirsting in his bowl,
dozes in the window.

In the kitchenette, I perch frog-like on a stool,
savoring the dusty mist
of tea.
Out in the open, the day is unlivable.

The clouds rain gasoline.

XI

He took me to the boiler room
nights
in our old building.
Sometimes a child later puts up searchlights

for the Father years absent.
Arms and legs lying scattered on the bed,
a sandy-skinned teenager
sighs and cries through all the wanting of that age.

He was a bad man.
I only wanted to see—his aquarium eyes.

XII

In the nameless, lightless twilight of a winter day,
children cut out paper snowflakes
studiously.
They decorate their tall classroom windows

with their knowledge of infinity.
Industrious, I spend the night gathering silky threads
dangling from the stars,
looping each filament around a button on my coat

until I am tethered to half of Heaven
and float up.

XIII

I look down Seventh Avenue
into the greasy distance
and understand:
I do not exist in that distance.

It is not quite the future
nor exactly the past
but an oblong moment
drifting back into view:

miles of stoplights
all turning at once.

XIV

Elsewhere, beyond the parking problem,
past smog rolling over fields,
in a truck stop diner in Ohio,
I wake to the blunt tolling of coffee cups.

In the little town off the road,
already wide awake under the dank horizon,
a young prisoner is pulled by the arm
into the courthouse. Across the dry lawn,

the shadows shorten until noon,
and green apples thud in the dust.

XV

When the river of summer has channeled
its last drop to the sea
let dreams blowing like leaves
run its dry course

so that open waters may grow fantastic
and the slow undertow of sleep
draw me into the inaudible deeps
to a meadow of black sand

and my white-cold horse.

XVI

I used to love a powder blue Mustang,
or I loved the Boy who drove it.
Sex came on me
suddenly like hot water in the shower.

We broke up, and I cried angrily,
a pair of tiny hurricanes circulating
in my coral eyes.
Pimples flared on my hot face like omens.

XVII

The Poet said he would protect me from wolves.
He always smelled of cock,
chased fire trucks, loved camera crews.
His manifestos were magpies:

intelligent, loud—lost in the underbrush.
He said death is an icy wind
streaming through a buttonhole.
He was quiet as a cancer.

He wore scarves of madness.

XVIII

I worship an unhappy god.
He sits alone
in a huge room full of light.
He himself worships stillness—

nonbeing.
His universe is a concussion,
and we are dark spots
dancing before his dazzled eyes.

XIX

My handbag tries to speak,
its hinged maw gaping.
No words come out,
but I know it's hungry—

it likes to taste things,
put objects in its mouth:
sticky dimes and pennies,
popcorn.

Neither could a baby speak.

XX

Fresh breath and white teeth
more popular every day,
I leer at my own modality
in the mirror of being and vogue.

Savvy, delicious impresarios
sacrifice virgins in the playhouses
behind velvet ropes.
I let my threadbare bath towel fall

and dress with dripping hair.

XXI

Everyone adored the flash and tonnage
of the shrapnel cathedral—
except the tender priest
with his rented koans and quiet loaves.

It was an era of bungling philosophers
who put their fingers in our ears.
I wore a microphone at my throat
in the shape of a cross

and could not stop talking.

XXII

The Hapax discusses mathematics dreamily,
dreams mathematically.
She is a rogue. Automaton!
She does not cherish universal laws

but hard-wires them in her wrists.
She digs mine shafts
in search of butterflies in the dark.
She wears her cardboard clothing nakedly.

Her logic is washable in cold water only.

XXIII

Grief on the Poet's forehead is a white desert,
an empty space on the map—
nowhere to go. No way to get there.
Here he is alone.

In the reflecting pool of his consciousness,
the turtles perform a slow ballet,
everything remembered balanced exactly
against everything forgotten.

For he knows—too much comforting
shrivels the blossom of crisis.

XXIV

Thorns grow from the Bearded Lady's flesh.
I help her pluck them.
There is a wet robin with us in the bath,
not very cheerful

in the soapy, blood-pink water.
On the windowsill, a spider skips as it walks.
Outside, beyond the moon-white fence,
we hear a girl crying softly,

sweetly to herself.

XXV

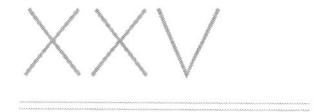

The land is leaking away.
Unrooted elms levitate uncertainly.
The earth dangerously shallow,
I can almost see through to the bottom.

A hive emerges from the under-ground
splitting open and spilling
honey and bees onto my feet.
I do not feel the stings

but stand transfixed like an anatomical model
encased in clear plastic flesh.

XXVI

The Poet is not real, even to himself,
except in his convex mirror.
His eyelashes are made of spiders' legs.
He has a trained starling for a smile.

Confidant of liars, comrade of sleepers,
he is a long warm orgasm
under heavy sheets. He squirts white ashes.
Dusty, he makes nothing out of even less.

XXVII

There were ten thousand louts in the rusty city.
I danced outdoors with two. The polka.
I was happy
in a happy crowd of painted beer steins.

But the city does in fact sleep,
and I woke gradually at dawn in my room
with no one but the dead bees on the windowsill
and dust motes

dancing an infinitesimal two-step.

XXVIII

The card player is endlessly calm.
A buzzard in a holding pattern a mile high,
he detects the ornate reek of guile,
a thought process come to its conclusion,

the mind rotting there,
and his own rapacious consciousness
begins to circle down.
Serene, he is tyrannized by the cards.

XXIX

A little bird with wires for legs,
kinked toes,
clutches the phone line,
taps in

but does not understand,
sings four notes of liquid song
impulsively—
then stops, cocked

to listen again to our beautiful voices.

XXX

In the long hallway of my building
I put my ear to doors
as though the silence behind each
were the stillness of a golden crypt.

At the end of the dark passage
evening amber sunbeams
blaze unexpectedly across the floor:
an open door. I pass through the light

like a heron walking in shallow water.

XXXI

All the children at reality school
have bloody noses.
They take disquieting naps,
their vulgar shoes lined up beside them.

They learn about the no smoking light,
fasten seatbelt light,
the frail wings of the jet,
the fragile wings of the deadly bee.

XXXII

I had claws on my feet
Einstein's blown-fuse hairdo
and insufficient neurons to control
my tingling earlobes

alarm clock heart
and across the blacked-out city
lights coming on in vast, banked choirs
and the Boy paralyzed,

an iron bridge arch bolt slipped loose.

XXXIII

By morning I believe in five gods,
or rather, not the gods
but the proofs, the pearled logic and satin synthesis,
the intimate visitation and shy testimony,

the vision, clarity, light,
the mighty hand
set gently on the mortal shoulder—
I believe

in the comforts of the lonely night.

XXXIV

The Hapax is rumored to ride the subway
only after midnight
when the uniformity of florescent dust-shine
most resembles the metallic dusk of her snowbound youth.

Others have it that she carries a dimmer switch
and dials down
the luminosity of other spirits
at will

and so passes innocently among us.

XXXV

Somewhere a dying child
wears a wig of my donated hair,
and under the trickling static
of the wiry red curls,

I imagine her wise,
mature beyond her possible years,
the vibrating lobes of her brain
instructing her urgently

to kiss her mother, father,
though she cannot move her lips.

XXXVI

My beach towel a chaotic rectangle of loose strings,
the sun a ferocious harlequin,
I sweat tar, spit
weed killer,

all the superheated atoms of my being jittering out of place.
The gulls
are like buddhas
lifted on sandy gusts. I am lifted by the surf

but look breathlessly back toward the leaning towers, the
    surgeries,
the luxury toilets of the city.

XXXVII

The memoirist is a false witness
weaving a dreary fairy-fable
of blood-spotted sheets
and vile kisses.

My princess is immune to the poison apples
handed out at the cruddy town tavern
and carries hers in circles proudly
biting the painful fruit.

XXXVIII

Saturday nights the cars hurl dirt across the track
onto a keen crowd burned red and brown
by combustion, endless tobacco, beer.
Their god is a gambler,

a loiterer under a string of yellow lightbulbs.
So too the drivers, haughty at twenty,
depend on love and luck.
Stopwatches disagree and start fistfights.

Homeward, there are ditches, room for us all.
But the best stars slide across the sky in retrograde.

XXXIX

Through a wrinkled pane of glass
the garden looks old.
The flower heads dangle like great thought
as one by one the exhausted bees rise in the still-hot sun

and for the last time orient themselves
and go.
Already the moths are gone—
the yellow ones, the white ones, twitching.

My restless yesterdays are gone.
There is a blade of grass on my shoe.

XL

The Boy went out in a butane shirt
with sleeves of blue flame
spent the hot night
sniffing crotches at the strip joint

and on his back tasting delicious feet
a cinnamon odor tingling
in one nostril
thickening on the tongue—fell asleep

under a blanket of floorboards
woke in wreckage.

XLI

Like schoolchildren with a project due tomorrow,
we'll have to start from scratch,
build yet another papier-mâché civilization,
and pray it doesn't rain.

We'll dress our men in cricket whites
and taut surgical masks.
The women will arrive on a kiddie-park train
with replacements.

All will speak the language of obelisk and pyramid
in the lax dialect of our misanthropy.

XLII

I loved only springtime,
so green were the trees of her lakeshores.
Even inside her fur coat
I found a willow branch budding.

In the summer she wore a gray and blue gown,
a thundercloud billowing,
and lightning flashed darkly between her legs.
Quickly red leaves flourished and fell from her fingertips.

When she caressed my cheek, I ached for her,
though her touch burned—like frostbite by a wincing fire.

XLIII

Lunch with the Poet is all about the hustle of conversation,
the elevated train and idling cabs,
dust motes blazing like suns above our streetside table,
the shadow of his fingers crossing my arm.

He believes in a separate heaven
for the unlucky,
theorizes about stump-limbed children smiling for the
    camera,
the humiliation of horses,

leads me by the wrist through the canopied rug market
of his Renaissance but vagabond mind.

XLIV

The Hapax sails continents
and discovers ships.
She commits crimes so beautiful
the weather cools.

Her earrings are made of black caviar.
Her decrees are costly cigars.
Her malice is enigmatic,
her kisses perilous.

She confronts the infinite
by telephone. Orders lunch flawlessly.

XLV

The Bearded Lady says a thousand prayers
mournfully every night,
falls asleep yearning for tomorrow's
buckets of rain.

As though struck blind in the sun
for her wish,
her eyes ogle and bulge in the morning,
and as we walk arm in arm in the garden,

bees with legs like black needles
gather the sleep-grains from her eyes.

XLVI

I erect bronze statues of my enemies,
one drinking vodka from a flask,
another sucking on the barrel of a gun,
a third getting into a cab,

the cabbie's glance in the rearview mirror
a white gash across the rolling cityscape
revealing the moist inner organs
of his anxiety,

a shoebox full of tongues, the blobs of bullets.

XLVII

The chandelier is the root of a magical tree. Upstairs,
in the shade of consciousness,
I contemplate a handful of sleeping pills.
I dream

Sand dunes beget dynasties of sand dunes.
Doughty children march in the snow.
I pull rolling luggage through endless airport corridors.
Marry a suave dictator.

Struggling with a math problem on the blackboard.
I hate myself.

XLVIII

The magnitude of a corpse
is measured by its scavengers,
the knots tied in its winding-sheets,
the pillars circling and dignifying

its humiliation,
the obliteration of spirit
by its own massive dwelling
crumbling in upon it.

XLIX

The Bearded Lady is a relentless, intricate friend.
Dance-drunk, she kneels in sickness.
A well-constructed chamber of suffering
protects her from further hurt.

Her limestone eyes are soft
after years of rain.
She goes home to a bed made of bricks
and dreams of exotic goats

who flaunt their pretty ribbons and precious locks
and flick their gray tongues indecently.

L

To whom does a god pray
to be reborn
as an emerald damselfly darting
over a field of irises?

In the windswept fire-pit of his mentality
smolder the ruins of history,
and what comfort
is the feeble warmth of his creation?

LI

I idolize the Hapax.
She calms her floating hair with a sapphire comb!
In her elfin embrace,
I feel with every nerve—her thistly eyelashes

stinging my cheek, her shadow bruising deeply
where it grips my arms,
the purple fingerprints a prickling reminder
of her operatic indifference.

LII

Children on the stoop nourish rudimentary secrets
about tongues.
The wrought-iron lamppost is naturally patient
and lunatic.

I pick up cigarette butts from the sidewalk.
Rustling in my palm,
they are like wasps. When one escapes,
sparrows attack it.

LIII

The Bearded Lady displays herself on a sofa
stuffed with hairbrushes.
A rawhide mirror reflects the odor
of her nakedness.

Slow eyelids strumming the air,
she eats and calmly vomits my white-cake friendship,
eats and calmly vomits
the eggshells and blisters of my resistance.

LIV

The Poet wears a suit made of teacups
in order to hear himself think.
Chance and volition both
painted his paisley wings just so.

His black shoes scarred in street battles,
he loves the opaque whiteness of the dishtowel,
the pomegranate's false, clear blood.
Groping in a drawer for a knife,

he seeks the absolute.

LV

The Boy's deformities require contradiction.
I must deny him.
His cracked fingers, hardened crookedly,
grip crookedly.

His feelings for me geared up in football pads,
his bed is a stadium
rusted down to the concrete slab,
old rose petals scattered like ticket stubs,

and I am a deaf, mistrustful lover.
I must deny him.

LVI

The ghost of girlhood is awake—
a nightgown walking barefoot
down the hall, through the mirrors,
faceless,

though we know she is afraid,
her future a slit vein.
In the street, rain roils all night.
She rides a bicycle made of bones.

A stallion grows in her womb,
a dark, unstoppable pulse.

LVII

My words are big shoes
clopping through painted caves,
my litany
a clanging crowbar in a burial vault.

My voice vibrates at the windy tips of spires
and surfs
the curl of air beneath a pigeon's wing.
But what if everything is told?

I will keep one secret
in the pink throat of the hollyhock flower.

LVIII

We are strange to the bees,
prismatic
and myriad, like droplets of sun and rain
colliding in the misty blue vistas of their heaven,

though profusion means everything to the sapient hive,
and they love the musical hairstyles of flowers,
minuet, gavotte,
even poorly imitated in our droning art.

LIX

Certainty comes naturally,
like swimming in a swift river.
Faith, a slum burned to the ground,
rebuilds.

Doubt takes practice, like chess
and love,
and I am a seagull stabbing a pill bottle on the beach:
I will never comprehend it.

LX

Time, that vandal, broke into our rented bungalow
and made off with all our immortality.
The Poet's eyes filled with an ocean of sleep,
and at sunset he regarded the beach

as both a wave and a particle.
The lantern of his drowsy scrutiny shed an amber light,
and with the tip of his pen he prodded bits of shell,
fish scales, quartz grains,

until all was broken down in the dark
and he cried.

LXI

We invented shames
for our dolls,
spread salmon-smeared thighs,
packed their lungs with wet clay.

We defiled the playground:
pocket full of pins,
necklace of hot match heads,
purple eyelids veering in flame.

LXII

I met the Boy on a hot tar roofscape
openly among the exhaust vents and broken bottles.
He gave me a lucky bracelet
made of needles.

Humidity spilled over us.
His lips tasted like double-A batteries,
tangy and electric,
and I was a tenement of blown lightbulbs and rattling window
    glass

shaking in his arms.

LXIII

The Poet stands in a hard, cold rain
under a granite umbrella,
head filled with the clangor
of grails and chains.

Our conversation through the mail slot
is clear
and elemental: milk, no milk,
love.

Not love. For on the inside I am cold—
black snow falling on a white rose.

LXIV

The Bearded Lady looks into the imposter's mirror
with the gaze of an amateur flirt—
uncertain.
Gospel is ecstasy,

but gravity is intimate.
I touch her imperfect breast,
my gaze
a moth posed attentively on her nape.

She turns—and her light kisses taste of ginger snaps.

LXV

The Poet leaves not a corpse
but his diary by the millpond in the park.
Bees loot the gardens in his absence.
A green stain smothers the pool.

He walks in the mirror world
beneath the water.
When he speaks,
broken coins rattle against his teeth,

though we hear nothing above the gunfire
and revolutionary hymns of the bees.

LXVI

The artist had time to paint the thief
death,
time to capture the bee, a globe spinning
among the clover flowers,

desperate time
for the bourbon buddha slumped on a park bench,
for jongleurs and buffoons,
the balloon peddler by the ranting fountain,

for the baby and her toothless scream,
for a dog yawning.

LXVII

The Hapax drives a glossy automobile
into a utility pole.
A gash on her forehead bleeds
tea and milk.

Her invulnerable smile shows all of her teeth:
they are in mint condition.
Getting out of the car is sudden.
She lurches into the street, still jazz-drunk,

and opens her phone—
though she has no friends.

LXVIII

Among cheap, wind-shaken housing blocks
stacked on vacant lots,
her apartment tower is a pyramid built of cameras
all flashing.

I wake to morning fog
in a landscape of shattered porcelain.
A silver radio in the kitchen
broadcasts the existential static of her absence.

Alone in the lair of the Hapax,
I burn my clothes in her diamond fireplace.

LXIX

I find the Hapax in the bathroom
nibbling pills.
My polite, antique cough does not disturb her.
I snap away her towel.

A pretty pink dragon tattooed on her translucent shoulder
glistens with fresh pinpricks of blood.
Her boiled hair
smells of lemon biscuits and chocolate.

My steel fingernails grind
against her mask.

LXX

Arriving on the scene in chrome stockings
and marching-boots,
I stand with the innocent on the sandy shore.
They can go no further.

I flinch, and the crust of my face flakes.
My surviving eye glares
with the oily residue of fulfilled desire.
Sunset a bronze idol

melting in the crucible of my cupped hands,
I wade into the bewildering white twilight.

LXXI

The intruder
wore my slippers
and braided my hair
despite my puzzled refusal

we bounced on plaid furniture
knocking over athletic trophies and
with the confident curiosity of little hobos
hopped a freight train full of cellos

and other cargo of the night
bound for the museum of stale hay and rutted roads.

LXXII

In the mirror of the Bearded Lady, I have golden lips.
My painted jaw opens like a music box,
and my eye is a green gemstone
alive with tendrils of light.

My moods are amber,
my laughter dry, like birch bark.
I wear only wool of the rarest colors—
though tarnished.

In my lewdly muscled stomach, a whirlpool of sickness
rises and falls.

LXXIII

I am not ruled
by a politburo of celebrities on TV
but by footage at eleven
of bullet casings and corpses

in a green courtyard,
for I am a sparrow
propelled by the gunpowder flash
of my hunger.

LXXIV

A fly buzzes righteously in a web of enshrined habit.
Devotees of bloated wealth
baptize each other in the sewage canals of the rich.
A dog licks the carcass of its pup.

Engorged with fear, a phalanx of police turns the corner.
Surprised, spurting,
they break a pilgrim's grasshopper crutches
and leave the manic flesh

to the reverent furnace of nature.

LXXV

An idea rattles in a jammed turnstile.
Another is a pigeon pecking at my shoe,
but I can't reach it,
or kick it away.

I buy the morning paper mutely.
My ear is a wine-soaked bottle bag,
and the bee creeping inside
smells the thick nectar

of my fecundity.

LXXVI

Black vinyl legs
and arms of white gauze,
cheeks plum and gold,
nose down, tersely

I sip the sterile cocktail
of my ambition,
saturating my body
with creamy tremors,

for I will have no truth
without passion.

LXXVII

Beyond the etched lenses of his eyes
the Poet thinks it's always raining.
In his briefcase
he carries a blueprint of himself.

His ornate destiny
is obscured by scaffolding and tarpaulins.
I approach him
shrieking, puffing, scissor-punctured—

He unbuckles his mouth to speak.

LXXVIII

Sleep, time's lazy accomplice,
caught up with me.
My closet was full of airplane wreckage.
Barges hauled confetti out to the sea dump.

I went to see the god again,
tried to renegotiate,
but he was impatient, a snarling clown
with chlorine breath and a vulture's hairline.

My footprints were tatters in the snow.
A mechanical canary chirped the hour.

LXXIX

Drawn to my room
by the dishonest fragrance of my bed,
a bee survives on the sill
without resolve.

Under the microscope of my careless scrutiny,
it is a glassy, dusty thing: intimate
and implacable,
agent of alarming fertility

and pain.

LXXX

I indulge the Bearded Lady—
the unutterable formality of her footsteps,
her cowl loneliness,
the gallows of her wooden shoulders.

Hers is a pewter energy, her witchcraft
lavender.
Her courage is a millstone
as she walks in misery to the healing well.

Her thousand deaths make me laugh
and not cry.

LXXXI

The Boy's frontal lobe
went over the falls in a barrel,
the river of his remaining
thought slowing

between banks of slag
and offal,
industry of his sub
cognition.

His body a safari of tattoos,
he is a nimble deer dodging javelins in the forest.

LXXXII

The Hapax is at once the hooded bride
and crested victor on the hotel balcony.
Her slitted skirt a pink evisceration,
she is all sinew and forbidden habit.

She jangles daring, bloody chains,
her future a spiral of incense smoke
and the gamble of animal sacrifice.
She sucks the hot exhaust pipe of love

and cries thumbtacks
in her marriage of jade and dynamite.

LXXXIII

I gather to my cheekbones
crabapple blossoms drenched in a cold drizzle.
I lick violets, kneeling obscenely,
and draw yellow dandelion heads into my mouth.

I want to taste what the bee tastes,
nectar and pollen, but more, her chemical imprint,
footprints on the petals,
to learn where she has been, what orchards and nurseries,

gardens, graves—
and if she ever blushes.

LXXXIV

Outside the baseball park, the city is a biohazard
attended by solemn men in jumpsuits,
while inside, a million clover flowers open for the bee
and ten thousand fans cheer.

Though his reflexes are glazed with salt and sand,
the Poet is still aroused by the game,
awed by the crowns and wreaths of the green stage,
the barefaced gods, the chrysanthemum prize,

but pricked most by the helmet and shield of defeat
and the fanfares of dented trumpets.

LXXXV

The Bearded Lady is a pony fattening in a gravel yard,
its winter coat a thick rind.
I produce a small vial of mean-streak
and dab my throat.

Reaching out to my old friend with a nacreous fingernail,
I cut her arm.
The Hapax, a lanky aviatrix in haute couture,
flings me a snide salute.

But what is love without plumage
or wind to lift it?

LXXXVI

The Bearded Lady dwells at the beach
in citrus light
and saffron contemplation
under an umbrella of brilliant blue foil

while the leaden rays of the sun
push me down
into a fierce carbon abyss
and catastrophic flexing of muscle.

LXXXVII

The Hapax is the last dot in a line of dots
plotted partway across the Arctic.
Her map
is otherwise all white.

In the wind-screaming stillness of her tent,
a linen napkin and glass pitcher
wait on the camp-table.
In the frying pan, potatoes blacken despondently.

LXXXVIII

I want to be like the Poet,
soft as damp moss dusted with funeral ash,
holy, indigo, colorfast, manicured.
Mercurial grandmaster of the cheat, lapse, and skid,

he calls me the sham of death,
a cut artery jittering like a lawn sprinkler,
an old mattress soaked in cold vinegar,
untouchable, fugitive, a docile and disfigured voice.

He throws down the bouquet of his contempt,
and I have never seen anything so beautiful.

LXXXIX

The Bearded Lady preens her blisters inconsolably.
She counts her ovaries, always perversely
stopping at one.
She looks at me through the mildewed lenses of her eyes

which roll with awkward yearning.
When she touches my face with her lustrous palm,
I notice her capsized halo
for the first time, and when she rights it,

the whole world is right.

XC

The Boy arrived in a purring suburban bus
inching through the city.
His rural inflections pressed flat,
I admired his flaxen silence.

We walked in a soft, disappointing storm.
His feelings for me increased in the rain
like a swollen marsh
from which great wading-birds rose.

XCI

Every time the Poet walks into a bar, someone
stabs him.
Threads of smoke rise from the wound
while his supply of iodine in corked bottles rattles in his
    pockets.

Every day he walks in the fields
tossing slippers and ribbons into bomb craters
and so every night drinks a cauldron of liquor without
    ceremony
or magic.

He bought stock in eternity on a hunch.
His old cuts wrinkle crookedly when he smiles.

XCII

Under the sun's placid scorching,
the beach in submissive repose,
the Poet sings of his preposterous affection
for a dead gull wreathed in black seaweed.

He plays a guitar made of shells and litter
surrounded by effigies of vacationers.
Street brawling postcards spill out of the souvenir kiosk.
Snow globes proliferate like white barnacles.

How egotistical and delirious his ice-cream magnanimity!
How I desire his cooling touch.

XCIII

I distrust sleep,
the liquidation of all assets,
but hazard a light eucalyptus nap
and with slow speech count silver lambs.

In the faint background noise of traffic twenty stories below,
I hear the wreck of two streamlined cabs,
pulp
in the lemonade metropolis.

Not until at the high window of my dreaming a lost
    spacefaring bee taps the glass
do I lift an eyelid.

XCIV

His brilliant flashbacks shrunken to the size of a dusty white
    pill,
the Poet hulks through a suffocating torpor.
His memories are smoky silhouettes riding the up-escalator—
they do not acknowledge him.

His happiest thoughts stand in the rain
at a lawn party.
He chuckles at his bestselling god, a surfer Einstein
riding a curl of gravity.

Then quite clearly he remembers
the first time someone held him under water.

XCV

The gluttonous queen
dines
on all the flowers of the countryside,
her table served by a lunging, trampling throng

who are themselves
no one
except they are like her, and like the fragrant palace itself,
made only of flowers.

XCVI

My turquoise-encrusted hand
breaks
against the side of the Boy's face
leaving exquisite white scratches, like marbled steak.

He wears a glove made of thistle leaves
and cupping the damaged cheek
greenly
props up his staggering, unendurable smile.

XCVII

The runaway looks like a depleted supermodel
smoking a life-giving cigarette.
She has worked herself all the way down
to this shoot in the alley.

Once, working down, she tried to murder zero,
that farce,
but the knife flew harmlessly
thru.

Unearthed, she is a muddy carcass in a swimsuit.
Then the rain starts, and the camera whirs.

XCVIII

Maybe after all there exists some barn-vast paradise
for the immaculate pigeon.
Maybe the cricket's scraped-together electricity
is a little epiphany ringing brightly through the summer night.

Startled awake under a wet raincoat,
endlessly hunted,
I smuggle corroded grave-trinkets,
a rusty ambulance creeping through the carnival

of my daring evasions.
Maybe when the tightrope of memory is cut—

XCIX

I share a ritual bath with the cat.
She is rightly concerned.
Lathered, pensive,
we soak

in warm grief.
For I am like the Poet's death-freckled protagonist:
He cannot permit her another day
and in his fury

hurls icy squalls splashing against the window.

In one version
I die surrounded by detestable cherubs
who hold down my arms
just outside the god's bright radius of immortality.

Or else I live on
chronicling the plagues and crop failures of my relationships
busily
while flocks of brown monks fly overhead

waving to me
bye.

Books Available from Gival Press
Poetry

Adamah by Céline Zins; translation by Peter Schulman
    ISBN 13: 978-1-928589-46-4, $15.00
    This bilingual (French/English) collection by an eminent French poet/writer is adeptly translated in this premiere edition.

Bones Washed With Wine: Flint Shards from Sussex and Bliss
by Jeff Mann
    ISBN 13: 978-1-928589-14-3, $15.00
    Includes the 1999 Gival Press Poetry Award winning collection. Jeff Mann is "a poet to treasure both for the wealth of his language and the generosity of his spirit."
    — Edward Falco, author of *Acid*

Canciones para sola cuerda / Songs for a Single String
by Jesús Gardea; English translation by Robert L. Giron
    ISBN 13: 978-1-928589-09-9, $15.00
    Finalist for the 2003 Violet Crown Book Award—Literary Prose & Poetry. Love poems, with echoes of Neruda à la Mexicana, Gardea writes about the primeval quest for the perfect woman.

Dervish by Gerard Wozek
    ISBN 13: 978-1-928589-11-2, $15.00
    Winner of the 2000 Gival Press Poetry Award / Finalist for the 2002 Violet Crown Book Award—Literary Prose & Poetry.
    "By jove, these poems shimmer."
    —Gerry Gomez Pearlberg, author of *Mr. Bluebird*

The Great Canopy by Paula Goldman
    ISBN 13: 1-928589-31-0, $15.00
    Winner of the 2004 Gival Press Poetry Award / 2006 Independent Publisher Book Award—Honorable Mention for Poetry
    "Under this canopy we experience the physicality of the body through Goldman's wonderfully muscular verse as well the analytics of a mind that tackles the meaning of Orpheus or the notion of desire."
    — Richard Jackson, author of *Half Lives*

Honey by Richard Carr
  ISBN 13: 978-1-928589-45-7, $15.00
  Winner of the Gival Press Poetry Award
  "Honey is a tour de force. Comprised of 100 electrifying microsonnets . . . The whole sequence creates a narrative that becomes, like the Hapax Legomenon, a form that occurs only once in a literature."
  —Barbara Louise Ungar, author of *The Origin of the Milky Way*

Let Orpheus Take Your Hand by George Klawitter
  ISBN 13: 978-1-928589-16-7, $15.00
  Winner of the 2001 Gival Press Poetry Award
  A thought provoking work that mixes the spiritual with stealthy desire, with Orpheus leading us out of the pit.

Metamorphosis of the Serpent God by Robert L. Giron
  ISBN 13: 978-1-928589-07-5, $12.00
  This collection "…embraces the past and the present, ethnic and sexual identity, themes both mythical and personal."
  —*The Midwest Book Review*

On the Altar of Greece by Donna J. Gelagotis Lee
  ISBN 13: 978-1-92-8589-36-5, $15.00
  Winner of the 2005 Gival Press Poetry Award / 2007 Eric Hoffer Book Award: Notable for Art Category
  "…*On the Altar of Greece* is like a good travel guide: it transforms reader into visitor and nearly into resident. It takes the visitor to the authentic places that few tourists find, places delightful yet still surprising, safe yet unexpected…."
  —by Simmons B. Buntin, editor of *Terrain.org* Blog

On the Tongue by Jeff Mann
  ISBN 13: 978-1-928589-35-8, $15.00
  "…These poems are …nothing short of extraordinary."
  —Trebor Healey, author of *Sweet Son of Pan*

The Nature Sonnets by Jill Williams
  ISBN 13: 978-1-928589-10-5, $8.95
  An innovative collection of sonnets that speaks to the cycle of nature and life, crafted with wit and clarity. "Refreshing and pleasing."
  — Miles David Moore, author of *The Bears of Paris*

The Origin of the Milky Way by Barbara Louise Ungar
ISBN 13: 978-1-928589-39-6, $15.00
Winner of the 2006 Gival Press Poetry Award
"…a fearless, unflinching collection about birth and motherhood, the transformation of bodies. Ungar's poems are honestly brutal, candidly tender. Their primal immediacy and intense intimacy are realized through her dazzling sense of craft. Ungar delivers a wonderful, sensuous, visceral poetry." —Denise Duhamel

Poetic Voices Without Borders edited by Robert L. Giron
ISBN 13: 978-1-928589-30-3, $20.00
2006 Writer's Notes Magazine Book Award—Notable for Art / 2006 Independent Publisher Book Award—Honorable Mention for Anthology
An international anthology of poetry in English, French, and Spanish, including work by Grace Cavalieri, Jewell Gomez, Joy Harjo, Peter Klappert, Jaime Manrique, C.M. Mayo, E. Ethelbert Miller, Richard Peabody, Myra Sklarew and many others.

Poetic Voices Without Borders 2, edited by Robert L. Giron
ISBN 13: 978-1-928589-43-3, $20.00
Featuring poets Grace Cavalieri, Rita Dove, Dana Gioia, Joy Harjo, Peter Klappert, Philip Levine, Gloria Vando, and many other fine poets in English, French, and Spanish.

Prosody in England and Elsewhere:
A Comparative Approach by Leonardo Malcovati
ISBN 13: 978-1-928589-26-6, $20.00
The perfect tool for the poet but written for a non-specialist audience.

Protection by Gregg Shapiro
ISBN 13: 978-1-928589-41-9, $15.00
"Gregg Shapiro's stunning debut marks the arrival of a new master poet on the scene. His work blows me away."
—Greg Herren, author of *Mardi Gras Mambo*

Songs for the Spirit by Robert L. Giron
ISBN 13: 978-1-928589-0802, $16.95
A psalter for the reader who is not religious but who is spiritually inclined. "This is an extraordinary book."
—John Shelby Spong

Sweet to Burn by Beverly Burch
ISBN 13: 978-1-928589-23-5, $15.00
Winner of the 2004 Lambda Literary Award for Lesbian Poetry Winner of the 2003 Gival Press Poetry Award — "Novelistic in scope, but packing the emotional intensity of lyric poetry..."
— Eloise Klein Healy, author of *Passing*

Tickets to a Closing Play by Janet I. Buck
ISBN 13: 978-1-928589-25-9, $15.00
Winner of the 2002 Gival Press Poetry Award
"…this rich and vibrant collection of poetry [is] not only serious and insightful, but a sheer delight to read."—Jane Butkin Roth, editor of *We Used to Be Wives: Divorce Unveiled Through Poetry*

Where a Poet Ought Not / Où c'qui faut pas by G. Tod Slone
(in English and French)
ISBN 13: 978-1-928589-42-6, $15.00
Poems inspired by French poets Léo Ferré and François Villon and the Québec poet Raymond Lévesque in what Slone characterizes as a need to speak up. "In other words, a poet should speak the truth as he sees it and fight his damnedest to overcome all the forces encouraging not to."

For a list of poetry published by Gival Press, please visit: *www.givalpress.com*.

Books available via Ingram, the Internet, and other outlets.

Or Write:
Gival Press, LLC
PO Box 3812
Arlington, VA 22203
703.351.0079